Lue Gim Gong
The Citrus Wizard

Christina Hill, M.A.

Consultants

Dorothy Levin, M.S.Ed., MBA
St. Lucie County Schools

Vanessa Ann Gunther, Ph.D.
Department of History
Chapman University

Cassandra Slone
Pinellas County Public Schools

Publishing Credits

Rachelle Cracchiolo, M.S.Ed., *Publisher*
Conni Medina, M.A.Ed., *Managing Editor*
Emily R. Smith, M.A.Ed., *Series Developer*
Diana Kenney, M.A.Ed., NBCT, *Content Director*
Courtney Patterson, *Multimedia Designer*

Image Credits: Cover and pp 1, 8, 9, 10, 12, 17 (top and bottom), 19 (top and bottom), 23, 25, 26 (left), 29 (middle), 31 Lue Gim Gong Collection, Special Collections Department, Tampa Library, University of South Florida, Tampa, Florida; pp. 6–7, 14–15 North Wind Picture Archives; pp. 7 (bottom), 13, 16, 32 Granger, NYC; p. 11 Picture History/Newscom; p. 15 OurDocuments. gov; p. 18 State Archives of Florida; p. 20 (back) inga spence/Alamy, (front) Len Wilcox/Alamy; p. 22 U.S. Department of Agriculture Pomological Watercolor Collection. Rare and Special Collections, National Agricultural Library, Beltsville, MD 20705; pp. 26 (right), p. 27 (left and right) Ebyabe/Wikimedia Commons; pp. 28–29 Linda Phillips/Science Source; all other images from iStock and/or Shutterstock.

Library of Congress Cataloging-in-Publication Data

Names: Hill, Christina, author.
Title: Lue Gim Gong, the citrus wizard / Christina Hill, M.A.
Description: Huntington Beach, CA : Teacher Created Materials, 2016. |
   Includes index.
Identifiers: LCCN 2016014369 (print) | LCCN 2016034195 (ebook) | ISBN
   9781493835492 (pbk.) | ISBN 9781480756960 (eBook)
Subjects: LCSH: Lue, Gim Gong, 1858 or 1859-1925--Juvenile literature. |
   Fruit growers--Florida--De Land--Biography--Juvenile literature. |
   Oranges--Florida--De Land--History--Juvenile literature. |
   Immigrants--Florida--Biography--Juvenile literature. |
   Chinese--Florida--Biography--Juvenile literature.
Classification: LCC SB63.L78 H55 2016 (print) | LCC SB63. L78 (ebook) | DDC
   641.309759--dc23

Teacher Created Materials

5301 Oceanus Drive
Huntington Beach, CA 92649-1030
http://www.tcmpub.com

ISBN 978-1-4938-3549-2
© 2017 Teacher Created Materials, Inc.

Table of Contents

Childhood in China

Around 1860, a baby was born in a small village in China. His parents named him Lue Gim Gong. Lue grew up on a farm. His mother taught him how to plant seeds and grow food. Lue **harvested** fruits and vegetables to sell at the market. But, Lue spent his childhood years longing for adventure.

Guangdong, China

rice field in South China

Last Name First?

In Chinese culture, family names come first. So *Lue* was really his last name. Lue's parents named him Gim Gong, which means "double brilliance." But when Lue came to the United States, people just assumed that Lue was his first name.

吕锦浓

Lue Gim Gong's name written with Chinese characters

When Lue was around 12 years old, his wish came true! His uncle returned from a trip to the United States. He had made money working in a gold mine. Lue was fascinated by his uncle's stories. Lue dreamed of traveling to the United States, too.

Lue asked his parents to let him go to this new place. He wanted to see it for himself. He wanted to go to school. His parents agreed after much thought. Lue boarded a boat and began the long journey to the United States.

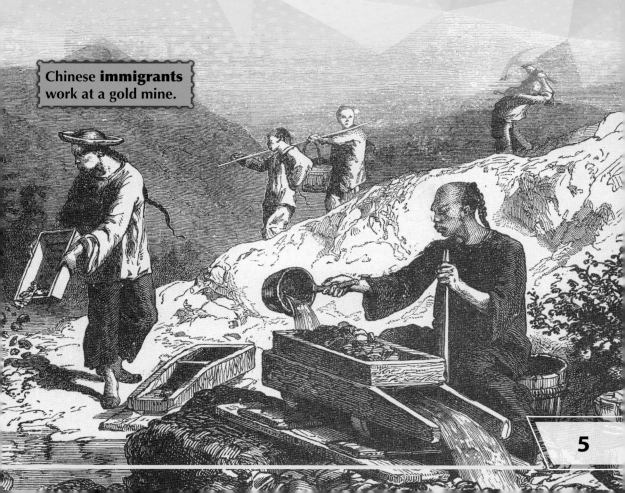

Chinese **immigrants** work at a gold mine.

Coming to America

Lue arrived in San Francisco in the early 1870s. Many Chinese workers had come there to build a railroad. They lived in Chinatown. This small section of the city was full of Asian immigrants and shops. They sold food and items that reminded Lue of home.

Lue began working in a shoe factory. He worked hard. He sent the money he made home to his parents. Later, he applied for a better paying job. It was in another shoe factory on the East Coast. Lue traveled by train all the way across the country.

Chinatown

In the 1850s, about 10,000 Chinese came to the United States. By 1867, about 50,000 lived in California. Many Chinese lived in San Francisco because of the available railroad jobs. There, they started a community called Chinatown.

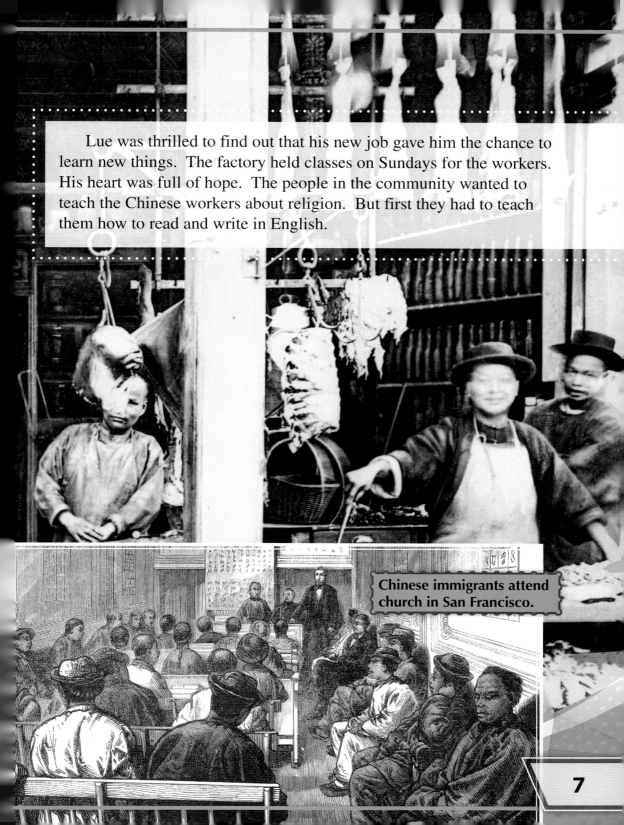

Lue was thrilled to find out that his new job gave him the chance to learn new things. The factory held classes on Sundays for the workers. His heart was full of hope. The people in the community wanted to teach the Chinese workers about religion. But first they had to teach them how to read and write in English.

Chinese immigrants attend church in San Francisco.

A Friend for Life

Lue met Fannie Burlingame in the church classes. Burlingame quickly saw his potential for learning. She became his tutor and his best friend. She was many years older than Lue, so he lovingly called her "Mother Fannie."

Burlingame home

Burlingame and Lue spent much of their time learning from each other. Lue told her stories about China and all he knew about farming. This gave her a great idea! Her father owned a store and was very successful. They also had a large home with an **orchard**. So, she asked Lue if he would come to live with her family. He could work in the orchard, and she could continue teaching him English. Lue was happy to move into their home. He felt like he was part of their family. Lue taught Burlingame all he knew about growing crops and harvesting. And she taught him how to live like the other people in the United States.

Burlingame and Lue

Lue loved his new life in the Burlingame home. He had his own room, and he had access to books of all kinds. Lue spent his days studying. He also worked hard in the orchard and garden. He began experimenting with the plants. He applied everything he had learned from his mother. Soon, the orchard and garden were blooming with flowers and new fruit!

Lue Gim Gong

Fannie Burlingame

Around 1886, Lue became sick. He developed a serious illness that compromised his health. He had a lung disease that people called **consumption**. It consumed the patient's whole body. Lue was so weak he could barely move. The doctor told Burlingame that the cold weather on the East Coast was not helping Lue get better. She was determined to save him. So, she sent Lue back to China. She hoped the warm weather and medicine there would help Lue recover. Sadly, the two friends said goodbye. They were not sure they would ever meet again. With a heavy heart, Lue sailed home to China. It had been many years since he had last seen his family.

This X-ray shows consumption, now known as tuberculosis.

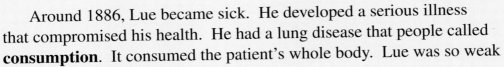

Anson Burlingame

The Burlingame Treaty

Fannie knew more about China than most people. Her cousin, Anson Burlingame, worked as a minister in China. He wanted the Chinese to be treated fairly. In 1868, the Burlingame Treaty was signed. It allowed Chinese and Americans to travel and trade freely between their countries.

Breaking Old Traditions

Lue went home to his family in China. His mother took care of him and made him soups full of healing **herbs**. Slowly, his health returned. But Lue was unhappy. He missed his life in the United States. His family did not understand his new appearance and the clothes he wore. They were upset that Lue had left his old religion for Christianity.

Guangdong, China

Lue's mother tried one last time to convince him to follow Chinese traditions. She bought him a bride. Lue was upset. He did not want to have an **arranged marriage**. He wanted to marry for love. And he was unsure of his health. He did not want to make his new wife a widow. He knew that if he said yes to the marriage, he would be forced to remain in China forever. So, he secretly wrote letters to Burlingame, begging her to help him go back to the United States.

a 1905 Chinese wedding photo

Arranged Marriage

In the past, many Chinese families arranged marriages for their children. Parents felt they could make the best choice for their children.

Going back to the United States would be hard. New laws had passed since Lue's first trip. These laws were passed to keep Chinese immigrants from entering the country. Only teachers, students, merchants, and diplomats were allowed to enter from China. But, Burlingame devised a plan. She sent Lue some money. Lue would pretend to be a merchant returning to the United States.

Chinese immigrants sail to San Francisco.

Lue was forced to make a tough decision. His family would **disown** him if he refused to follow Chinese tradition and get married. But he was certain he would never be happy if he stayed in China. Lue felt torn between two worlds. But he had to do what he felt was right for him. Lue fled on the morning of his wedding day. He boarded a ship bound for the United States and left his old life behind once again. His family would be left to face dishonor and shame. Sadly, they never spoke to Lue again.

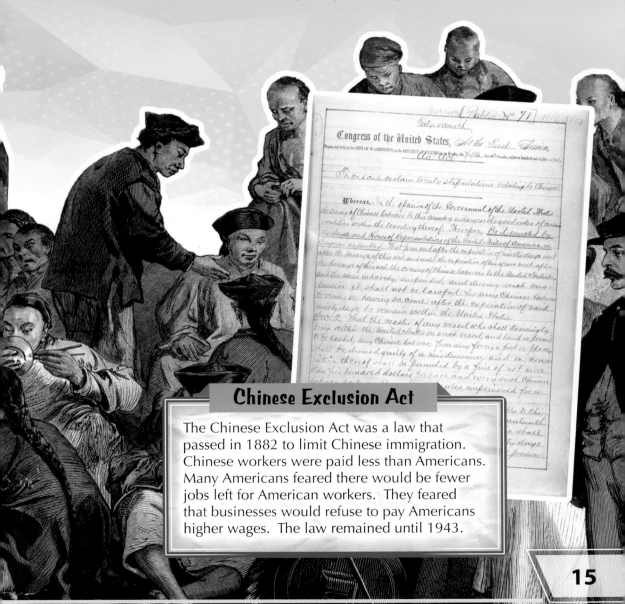

Chinese Exclusion Act

The Chinese Exclusion Act was a law that passed in 1882 to limit Chinese immigration. Chinese workers were paid less than Americans. Many Americans feared there would be fewer jobs left for American workers. They feared that businesses would refuse to pay Americans higher wages. The law remained until 1943.

The Struggle to Belong

Lue received a message from Burlingame's family as he traveled from China to the United States. The letter asked Lue to come to Florida. They had bought an orange **grove** in DeLand, Florida. They wanted Lue's help working on the land. Lue arrived in DeLand in December of 1886. This town would be his home for the rest of his life.

Things were different in DeLand. Lue was treated like an outsider. The people in the town were not kind to him because he was different. It was not considered proper for him to share a home with Burlingame there. So he lived on land separate from the family. He spent his days helping around the house and working in the fields. At night, he sat with Burlingame on the porch. He talked about his experiments with the fruit trees in the fields.

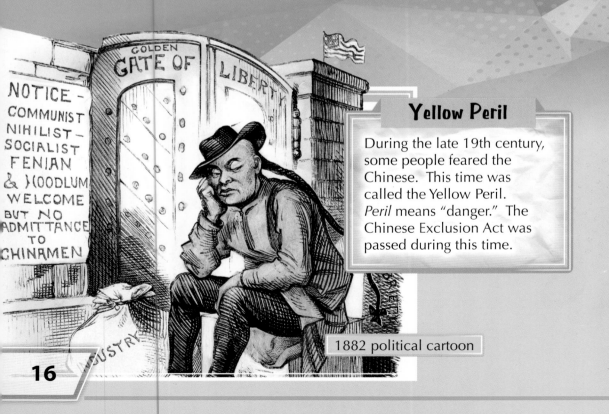

Yellow Peril

During the late 19th century, some people feared the Chinese. This time was called the Yellow Peril. *Peril* means "danger." The Chinese Exclusion Act was passed during this time.

1882 political cartoon

DeLand, Florida

Lue and Burlingame

DeLand house

17

Burlingame tried to help Lue adjust to life in the United States. Lue became a U.S. citizen around 1877. But even though he was a citizen, he still faced **racism**. People in DeLand had never met anyone from China. Being a citizen did not change that. Many people did not know what to think of him.

The years passed and Burlingame grew old. She became sick and died in 1903. Her death was hard on Lue. He lost his best and only friend. He had worked on her land for years but never received any wages. Lue had no home, no friends other than the Burlingames, and no money when she died. The Burlingames agreed to give Lue the property in DeLand. He decided to focus the rest of his life and energy to the one passion he had left—his citrus trees.

Lue's Beloved Pets

Lue had two horses named Fannie and Baby. He spoke to them like they were his children. Lue also had a pet rooster named March. His rooster sat on his shoulder and even joined him at the dinner table!

Perfecting the Orange

Lue studied the weather in Florida during his time there. He looked for trends, or patterns. Lue noticed that winters were getting colder each year. He **predicted** that a severe frost would soon hit. A frost can destroy many crops. Other farmers thought Lue was worrying over nothing. Florida was known for its mild weather. But Lue wanted to plan ahead. So, he began to experiment. He wanted to create a frost-resistant orange.

This is an orange with frost damage.

Lue's mother had taught him about **cross-pollination**. This is when pollen is taken from one plant and mixed with pollen from another plant. It can create a new type of seed that is a mixture of both plants. Lue chose to cross two different orange trees together. Then, he planted the new seeds. After tending to the trees for many years, the new fruit blossomed. It was sweet and tasty. Lue continued to work hard to perfect his oranges.

cross-pollination

Lue's prediction was correct. Winters got colder and a severe frost came. Many farmers lost all of their crops. But Lue's new oranges survived! His oranges were sweet and long-lasting. They could stay on the trees for three years before being harvested. And Lue's oranges ripened later in the citrus season. This meant he could sell his oranges at a time when there were few oranges available. The Lue Gim Gong orange was a success!

U.S. Department of Agriculture 1910 watercolor of the Lue Gim Gong orange

Lue's Oranges

Have you ever eaten a Lue Gim Gong orange? You probably have but didn't know it. Today, his oranges are known as Valencia oranges. Lue's oranges are still grown in Florida and California.

Lue applied what he learned to other fruit. He grew a new kind of grapefruit. He cross-pollinated a grapefruit and an orange that could survive the cold. Instead of clusters, he grew one grapefruit per branch. This kept the tree branches from being too heavy. He also created new apples and peaches that ripened at different times of the year. Other farmers came to Lue's home to learn about his growing methods. Lue became a teacher to those around him.

Lue Gim Gong

Awards, Achievements, and Acceptance

Years passed and Lue grew older. He lived a simple life. In 1911, Lue's lifetime of hard work paid off. He received the Silver Wilder Medal for his work in developing citrus. This award meant a lot to him. He was finally recognized for his work. His new methods of growing citrus were influencing the world.

Newspapers wrote stories about Lue. Writers called him "the Citrus Wizard." He no longer spent his days alone. Many people came to visit him and tour his gardens. Lue sent them home with oranges as gifts. People told stories about how kind and honest he was. One year, Lue didn't have enough money to pay his bills. A magazine editor wrote a story about him. He begged readers to help save Lue's grove. Readers responded and bought **bonds** to cover the new mortgage on the land. Lue was no longer an outsider. He was valued and accepted by his community.

Silver Wilder Medal

Too Kind

Lue was honest and generous but he did not understand how to run a business. Many people took advantage of him financially. At one point, he had over 200 debts that he was unable to pay.

newspaper articles about
Lue Gim Gong

Lue Gim Gong died in June 1925. People who had met him praised his kind spirit. They spoke about his courage. Lue followed his dreams and worked hard to achieve them. In doing so, he became a role model. He paved the way for other young Chinese immigrants.

LUE GIM GONG
THE
CITRUS WIZARD
1860 - 1925

Lue is remembered for his favorite saying, "No one should live in this world for himself alone, but to do good for those who come after him." And that is the legacy that Lue left behind.

It took years for Lue's work to become famous. His research was praised at two World's Fairs. At last, people began to see the importance of his citrus trees. Today, Florida **produces** 70 percent of the citrus fruit grown in the country. The fruit is a huge part of the state's **economy**. Lue's oranges are still loved by many! The work of one immigrant child from China continues to impact our world.

Lue Gim Gong Memorial Garden

The Henry DeLand House is now a museum in Florida. Visitors can learn more about the history of DeLand and "the Citrus Wizard."

Grow It!

Now it is your turn to grow an orange tree, just like Lue Gim Gong!

Materials

- Valencia oranges
- paper cups
- plastic sandwich bags
- paper towels
- water

Procedure

1. Dissect the orange. Remove the peel, and split the orange into wedges. Remove the seeds.

2. Write your observations. What do you see? How many seeds are there? How does it smell? How does it feel? How does it taste?

3. Wash the seeds with water.

4. Fill the paper cup with water, and let the seeds soak in the cup overnight.

5. Remove the seeds from the cup, and place them on a damp paper towel. Fold the paper towel to cover the seeds.

6. Place the bundle in the plastic bag. Keep the bag in a sunny location, such as a windowsill.

7. Inspect the seeds every few days. Record your observations. Add water to the paper towel if it dries out.

8. How long did it take your seeds to sprout? Record your observations. Share your observations with your family.

Glossary

arranged marriage—a marriage in which the husband and wife are chosen for each other by their parents

bonds—documents that promise to pay back an amount of money owed

consumption—a disease called tuberculosis that affects the lungs

cross-pollination—transfer of pollen from one plant to another to create a new plant

disown—decide to no longer be associated with someone

economy—the system of buying and selling goods and services

grove—a group of trees

harvested—gathered or collected a crop

herbs—plants used as medicine or to flavor food

immigrants—people who come to a country to live there

orchard—land where fruit trees are grown

predicted—said that something might happen in the future

produces—makes

racism—poor treatment because of race

Index

Your Turn!

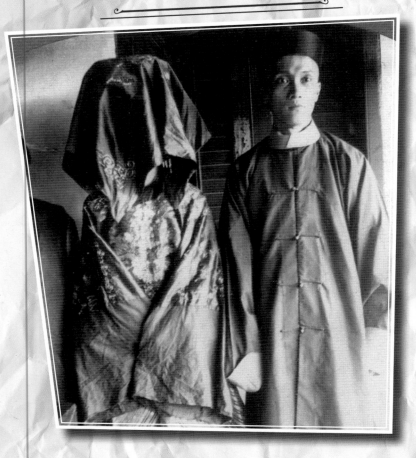

Wedding Photo

In traditional Chinese weddings, brides wear a red silk wedding veil. The color red represents happiness. In the past, brides wore the veil to hide their "shyness." Today, it is worn as a traditional keepsake. What traditions does your culture have? Choose one tradition and research its history. Create a Venn Diagram to compare and contrast the history with the modern-day practice.